MONEY MATTERS

Counting Coins

Financial Literacy

Michelle Jovin, M.A.

Consultants

Colene Van Brunt
Math Coach
Hillsborough Public County Schools

Publishing Credits

Rachelle Cracchiolo, M.S.Ed., *Publisher*
Conni Medina, M.A.Ed., *Managing Editor*
Dona Herweck Rice, *Series Developer*
Emily R. Smith, M.A.Ed., *Series Developer*
Diana Kenney, M.A.Ed., NBCT, *Content Director*
June Kikuchi, *Content Director*
Susan Daddis, M.A.Ed., *Editor*
Karen Malaska, M.Ed., *Editor*
Kevin Panter, *Senior Graphic Designer*

Image Credits: All images from iStock and/or Shutterstock.

Library of Congress Cataloging-in-Publication Data

Names: Jovin, Michelle, author.
Title: Money matters : counting coins / Michelle Jovin, M.A.
Description: Huntington Beach, CA : Teacher Created Materials, [2018] |
  Includes index. |
Identifiers: LCCN 2017055024 (print) | LCCN 2017058100 (ebook) | ISBN
  9781480759848 (eBook) | ISBN 9781425856908 (pbk.)
Subjects: LCSH: Money--Juvenile literature. | Coins--Juvenile literature.
Classification: LCC HG221.5 (ebook) | LCC HG221.5 .J68 2018 (print) | DDC
  332.4/0430973--dc23
LC record available at https://lccn.loc.gov/2017055024

Teacher Created Materials
5301 Oceanus Drive
Huntington Beach, CA 92649-1030
www.tcmpub.com

ISBN 978-1-4258-5690-8
© 2019 Teacher Created Materials, Inc.
Printed in China
Nordica.042018.CA21800320

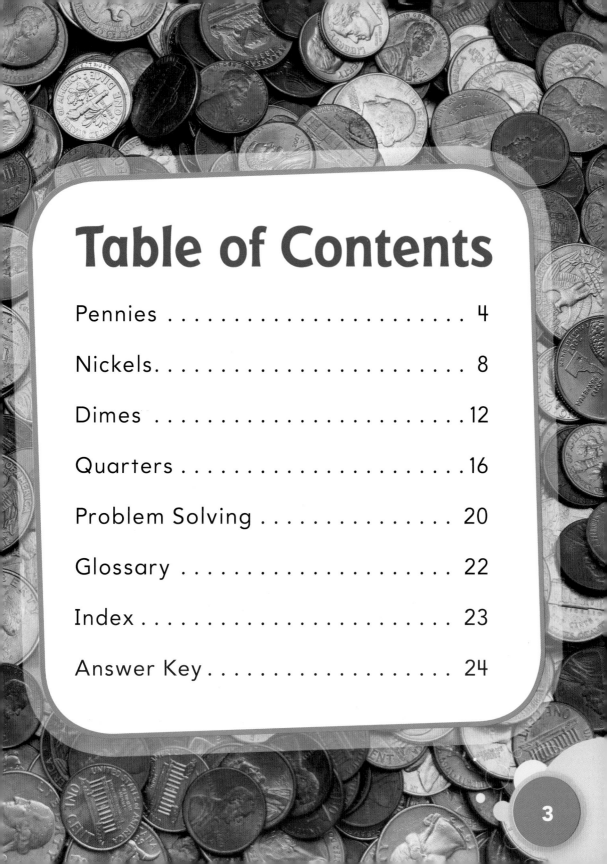

Table of Contents

Pennies

We use **coins** to buy things.

The coin **worth** the least is called a penny. It is a **copper** color.

One penny has a value of 1 cent. We write 1 cent as 1¢.

 = 1¢

How many pennies are there? Five pennies **equal** 5¢.

$+$

___

5¢

Nickels

The next coin is a nickel. It is larger in size than a penny. Its value is more, too.

One nickel has a value of 5 cents. We write 5 cents as 5¢.

How many nickels are there? Two nickels equal 10¢.

$= 5¢$

$+$ $= 10¢$

Kay is doing **chores**. While cleaning, she finds coins in the couch cushions. Count Kay's coins to solve the problems.

1. Kay finds _____ pennies. The pennies have a value of _____¢.

2. Kay finds _____ nickels. The nickels have a value of _____¢.

3. How did you find the value of Kay's nickels?

Dimes

The next coin is a dime. It is smaller in size than a nickel. But its value is more.

One dime has a value of 10 cents. We write 10 cents as 10¢.

How many dimes are there? Five dimes equal 50¢.

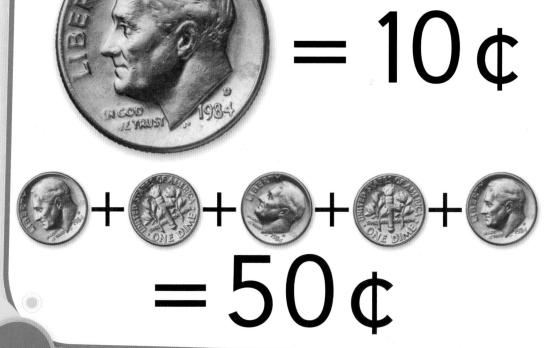

= 10¢

+ + + + = 50¢

Misu goes to the candy store. He has coins to **spend**. Count Misu's coins to solve the problems.

Misu has _____ dimes. They have a value of _____¢.

1. How did you find the value of Misu's dimes?

2. How many pennies have the same value as Misu's dimes? How do you know?

Quarters

The next coin is a quarter. Quarters are larger in size than the other coins. Their value is more than the other coins, too.

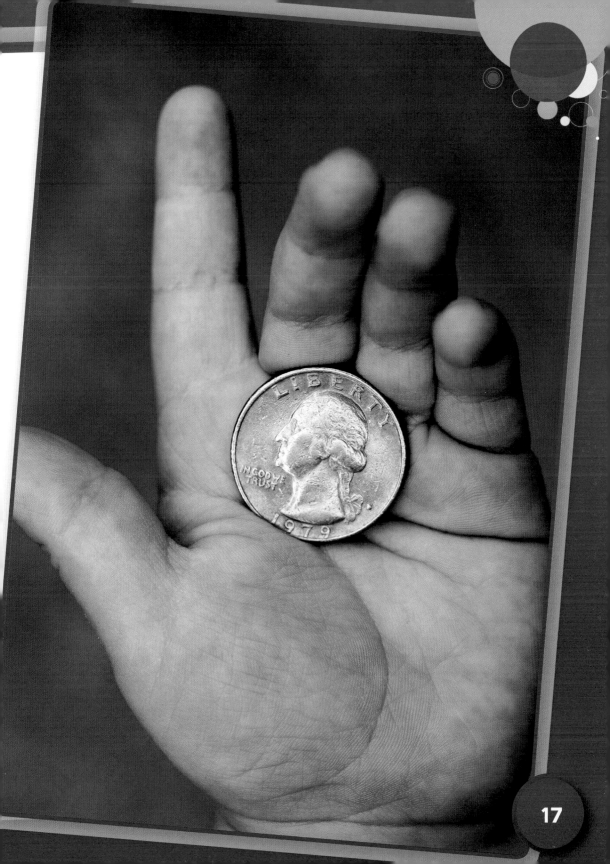

One quarter has a value of 25 cents. We write 25 cents as 25¢.

 $= 25$¢

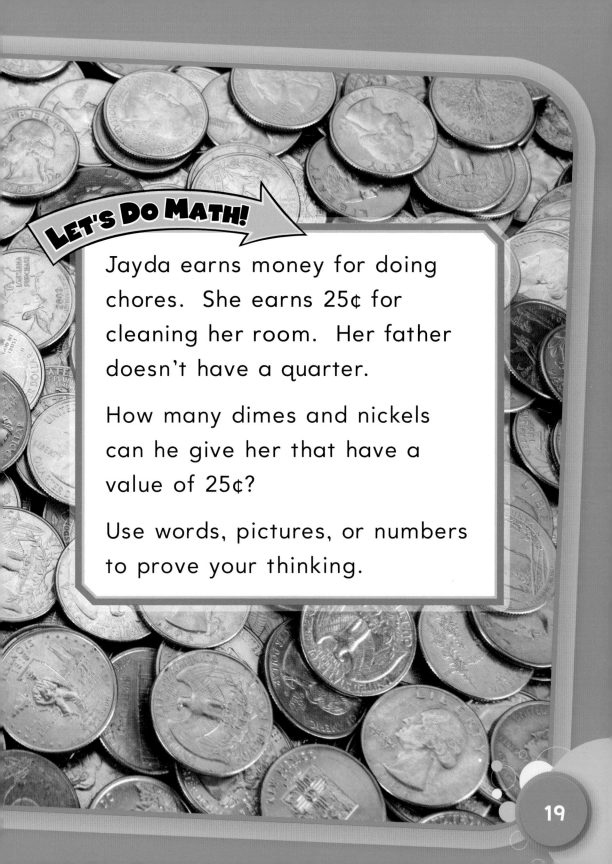

Jayda earns money for doing chores. She earns 25¢ for cleaning her room. Her father doesn't have a quarter.

How many dimes and nickels can he give her that have a value of 25¢?

Use words, pictures, or numbers to prove your thinking.

⚙️ Problem Solving

Bert keeps a jar of coins. Help him find the value of each set of coins. Then, answer the questions.

Coin	Number of Coins	Value
penny		
nickel		
dime		
quarter		

1. How did you find the value of each set of coins?

2. What is the total value of all the coins?

Glossary

chores—jobs that are often done around the house

coins—metal money

copper—a reddish-brown color

equal—the same as

spend—to pay money for something

worth—equal in value to

Index

Answer Key

Let's Do Math!

page 11:

1. 8 pennies, 8¢

2. 3 nickels, 15¢

3. counting by 5s

page 15:

4 dimes, 40¢

1. counting by 10s

2. 40 pennies; 40 pennies have a value of 40¢

page 19:

Answers will vary. Example: 2 dimes and 1 nickel

Problem Solving

penny—5, 5¢

nickel—3, 15¢

dime—2, 20¢

quarter—1, 25¢

1. counting by 1s, 5s, and 10s

2. 65¢